The Story of
THE CREATION
from the Book of Moses

DANIEL AND REBECCA RIDGES JENSEN

ISBN 13: 978-1-4621-4040-4

Published by CFI, an imprint of Cedar Fort, Inc.
2373 W. 700 S., Springville, UT, 84663
Distributed by Cedar Fort, Inc., www.cedarfort.com

LIBRARY OF CONGRESS CATALOGING-IN-PUBLICATION DATA

Jensen, Rebecca Ridges.
The Story of the creation / Rebecca Ridges Jensen and Daniel Loran Jensen.
p. cm.
ISBN 978-1-55517-894-9 (alk. paper)
1. Creation--Juvenile literature. 2. Church of Jesus Christ of Latter-day Saints--Doctrines--Juvenile literature. I. Jensen, Daniel Loran. II. Title.

BX8643.C75J46 2007
231.7'65--dc22

2006101308

Cover and book design by Nicole Williams
Cover design © 2021 by Cedar Fort Publishing
Edited by Annaliese B. Cox
Photographs on jacket, and pages 4, 5, 8, 9, 14, 30, and 31 courtesy of NASA, STScI, and hubblesite.org
Photograph on page 11 courtesy of USGS
Printed on acid-free paper

Printed in the United States of America
10 9 8 7 6 5 4 3 2 1

DEDICATION

TO OUR CHILDREN

WE MUST BE CAREFUL NOT TO UNDERESTIMATE THE CAPACITY OF CHILDREN TO READ AND TO UNDERSTAND THE WORD OF GOD.

—PRESIDENT THOMAS S. MONSON, "HALLMARKS OF A HAPPY HOME," *ENSIGN*, NOVEMBER 1988, 69

Intelligences

We were these intelligences who had been born as spirit children of our Heavenly Parents.

Noble and Great Ones

We were some of these noble and great ones, some of Heavenly Father's strongest children. He sent us to earth at this time to help prepare the earth for the Second Coming of Jesus Christ.

One among Them that was Like unto God

This was Jesus Christ.

✶⁺ Of These Materials
Jesus used His power to organize things like dust, gas, and water vapor that were already in space and bring them together to form the earth, sun, moon, and stars.

✶⁺ Prove Them Herewith
To "prove" means to test. This means that our life on earth is a test to see if we'll do what's right. This book tells the story of the creation of our wonderful world the way Jesus told it to the prophet Moses more than three thousand years ago.

LONG AGO, God planned the creation of our world. The prophet Abraham tells us this:

Now the Lord had shown unto me, Abraham, the INTELLIGENCES that were organized before the world was; and among all these there were many of the NOBLE AND GREAT ONES;

And God saw these souls that they were good, and he stood in the midst of them, and he said: These will I make my rulers; for he stood among those that were spirits, and he saw that they were good; and he said unto me: Abraham, thou art one of them; thou wast chosen before thou wast born.

And there stood ONE AMONG THEM THAT WAS LIKE UNTO GOD, and he said unto those that were with him: We will go down, for there is space there, and we will take OF THESE MATERIALS, and we will make an earth whereon these may dwell;

And we will PROVE THEM HEREWITH, to see if they will do all things whatsoever the Lord their God shall command them. (Abraham 3:22–25)

I Am the Beginning and the End

God is the beginning because He created all things (see Mosiah 4:9). He is the end because if we do our best to keep His commandments and follow Jesus Christ, we can return to live with Him forever in the end (see Alma 12:33–34).

Almighty God

This means that Heavenly Father has power over all things in heaven and also on the earth. He has the power to carry out His plan (see Mosiah 4:9).

Only Begotten

This is another name for Jesus Christ. Jesus created the earth, sun, moon, and stars in the way Heavenly Father told Him to as part of Heavenly Father's plan for us.

I AM THE BEGINNING AND THE END, THE ALMIGHTY GOD; by mine ONLY BEGOTTEN I created these things; yea, in the beginning I created the heaven, and the earth upon which thou standest. (Moses 2:1)

AND THE earth was WITHOUT FORM, AND VOID; and I caused DARKNESS to come up upon the face of the deep; and MY SPIRIT MOVED UPON THE FACE OF THE WATER; for I AM GOD. (Moses 2:2)

✳⁺ Without Form, and Void

When the earth was first made, it didn't have all the mountains, valleys, rivers, lakes, continents, and islands that it has now, and nothing lived on it. It was empty, or void (see Abraham 4:2).

✳⁺ Darkness

There wasn't any light shining on the earth yet to warm it and make it so things could grow and live here.

✳⁺ My Spirit Moved upon the Face of the Water

This means that Jesus was watching over the creation of the earth, to make sure things went the way they should, as part of Heavenly Father's plan (Abraham 4:2 calls it "brooding"—the same way a mother hen watches over her baby chicks).

✳⁺ I Am God

Jesus reminds Moses and us that He is a God, and that means that He has the power to carry out Heavenly Father's plan.

✳⁺ Divided the Waters

The water that was on the earth was divided.

Clouds and water vapor are called "the waters which were above the firmament" because they are above part of the sky.

The sky is called "the firmament."

Water on the surface of the earth is called "the great waters under the firmament."

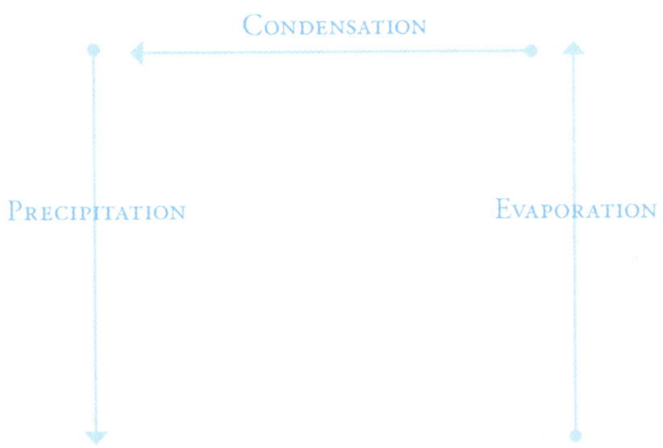

The water cycle keeps the waters divided so that we have the fresh water we need to live.

All living things that we know of need water, so this was an important part of getting the earth ready for us.

✳⁺ Heaven

Here, heaven means sky, not the heaven where good people go after they die, or where Heavenly Father lives (see Moses 2:8, footnote a).

AND AGAIN, I, God said: Let there be a firmament in the midst of the water, and it was so, even as I spake; and I said: Let it divide the waters from the waters; and it was done;

And I, God, made the firmament and DIVIDED THE WATERS, yea, the great waters under the firmament from the waters which were above the firmament, and it was so even as I spake.

And I, God, called the firmament HEAVEN; and the evening and the morning were the second day. (Moses 2:6–8)

And I, God, said: Let the waters under the heaven be gathered together unto one place, and it was so; and I, God, said: Let there be dry land; and it was so.

And I, God, called the dry land Earth; and the gathering together of the waters, called I the Sea; and I, God, saw that all things which I had made were good. (Moses 2:9–10)

✶⁺ Waters . . . Gathered together and Dry Land

Here Jesus made the waters come together into oceans, and dry land appeared so that there would be a place for plants, animals, and people to live.

AND I, God said: Let the earth bring forth grass, the HERB YIELDING SEED, the fruit tree yielding fruit, AFTER HIS KIND, and the tree yielding fruit, whose seed should be in itself upon the earth, and it was so even as I spake.

And THE EARTH BROUGHT FORTH grass, every herb yielding seed after his kind, and the tree yielding FRUIT, WHOSE SEED SHOULD BE IN ITSELF, after his kind; and I, God, saw that all things which I had made were good;

And the evening and the morning were the third day. (Moses 2:11–13)

✶⁺ Herb Yielding Seed

Here, "herb" just means plant. Plants make, or yield, seeds so that more plants can grow when the first plant dies. Jesus created plants and trees before He created the animals so that the animals would have the food they need to live as well as places to live.

✶⁺ After His Kind

This means that the seeds from a plant or tree will grow into that same kind of plant or tree. For example, an apple seed won't grow into a daisy. It will grow into an apple tree.

✶⁺ The Earth Brought Forth

The earth obeys Jesus and Heavenly Father in everything they command it to do. It provides everything necessary for plants and animals to live on it.

✶⁺ Fruit Whose Seed Should Be in Itself

This means that fruits have their seeds inside them.

Lights . . . in Heaven

This is our solar system and all the stars. The beauty and order of this solar system show us that God created it. In the Book of Mormon, the prophet Alma explained this to a man named Korihor, who asked to see a sign that there is a God. Alma said:

"All things denote there is a God; yea, even the earth, and all things that are on the face of it, yea, and its motion, yea, and also all the planets which move in their regular form do witness that there is a Supreme Creator" (Alma 30:44).

And I, God, said: Let there be lights in the firmament of the heaven, to divide the day from the night, and let them be for signs, and for seasons, and for days, and for years;

And let them be for lights in the firmament of the heaven to give light upon the earth; and it was so. (Moses 2:14–15)

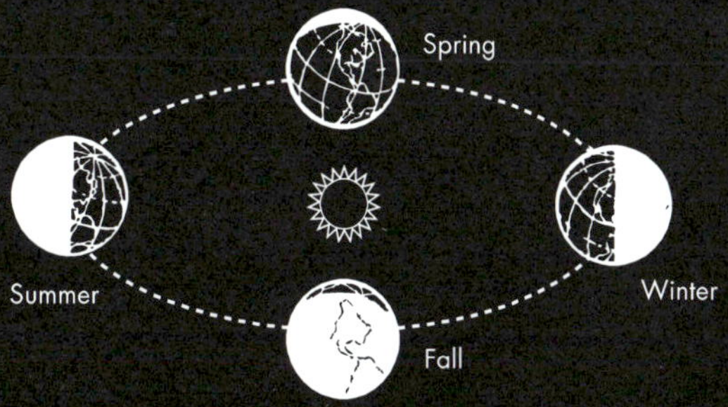

MARCH						
S	M	T	W	TH	F	SA
			1	2	3	4
5	6	7	8	9	10	11
12	13	14	15	16	17	18
19	20	21	22	23	24	25
26	27	28	29	30	31	

✶⁺ For Signs

Heavenly Father can sometimes use lights in heaven for signs of something important happening, like the new star in the sky or when it stayed light all night in America when Jesus was born (see 3 Nephi 1:15–21). Also, for thousands of years sailors used the position of the sun, moon, and stars to tell where they were.

✶⁺ For Seasons

Jesus made the earth so that it was tilted on its axis. That way the sun would shine on the earth at just the right angle to give us the four seasons: spring, summer, fall, and winter.

✶⁺ For Days, and for Years

We are able to keep track of time using the movements of the earth, sun, moon, and stars.

AND I, God, made two great lights; the greater light to rule the day, and the lesser light to rule the night, and the greater light was the sun, and the lesser light was the moon; and the stars also were made according to my word.

And I, God, set them in the firmament of the heaven TO GIVE LIGHT UPON THE EARTH. (Moses 2:16–17)

AND THE sun to RULE OVER the day, and the moon to rule over the night, and to DIVIDE THE LIGHT FROM THE DARKNESS; and I, God, saw that all things which I had made were good;

And the evening and the morning were the fourth day. (Moses 2:18–19)

✶⁺ To Give Light upon the Earth

Jesus made the sun, moon, and stars so that we would have light to see by and the warmth we need to live. Plants also use light to make food in a process called photosynthesis. Plants then become food for other living things, including people.

✶⁺ Rule Over

Here, this means "provide light for."

✶⁺ Divide the Light from the Darkness

Jesus made the earth rotate every 24 hours so that we would have the periods of daylight and darkness that we would need for work, play, and rest.

AND I, God, said: Let the WATERS BRING FORTH ABUNDANTLY the moving creature that hath life, and fowl which may fly above the earth in the open firmament of heaven.

And I, God, created great whales, and every living creature that moveth, which the waters brought forth abundantly, after their kind, and every winged FOWL AFTER HIS KIND; and I, God, saw that all things which I had created were good.

And I, God, blessed them, saying: BE FRUITFUL, AND MULTIPLY, and fill the waters in the sea; and let fowl multiply in the earth;

And the evening and the morning were the fifth day. (Moses 2:20–23)

✶ Waters Bring Forth Abundantly

Abundantly means "so that there is plenty." This means that the water on the earth will have plenty of fish, plants, and other kinds of life in it.

✶ Fowl

This is another word for birds. Jesus created the birds during the same period of time that He created ocean life.

✶ After Their Kind

Jesus made it so that each animal has babies that are the same kind of animal as the parents. Whales have baby whales, starfish have baby starfish, robins have baby robins, and so forth.

✶ Be Fruitful, and Multiply

Jesus commanded the sea creatures and the birds to have babies and fill the waters and the sky with wonderful living creatures.

AND I, God, said: Let the earth bring forth the living creature AFTER HIS KIND, CATTLE, and CREEPING THINGS, and BEASTS OF THE EARTH after their kind, and it was so;

And I, God, made the beasts of the earth after their kind, and cattle after their kind, and everything which creepeth upon the earth after his kind; and I, God, saw that all these things were good. (Moses 2:24–25)

✶⁺ After His Kind
Just like the plants and the birds and fish, each animal's babies will be the same kind of animal as the parents.

✶⁺ Cattle
Today, we usually think of cows when we hear this word, but here it means all large animals that people use, such as cows, goats, pigs, sheep, yaks, llamas, and others.

✶⁺ Creeping Things
Think of bugs, salamanders, snakes, worms, and all of the wonderful little creatures that Jesus has made.

✶⁺ Beasts of the Earth
This is another way to say animals.

AND I, God, said unto mine ONLY BEGOTTEN, WHICH WAS WITH ME FROM THE BEGINNING: Let us MAKE MAN IN OUR IMAGE, after our likeness; and it was so. And I, God, said: LET THEM HAVE DOMINION over the fowl of the air, and over the cattle, and over all the earth, and over every creeping thing that creepeth upon the earth. (Moses 2:26)

✶⁺ ONLY BEGOTTEN . . . FROM THE BEGINNING

The Only Begotten is Jesus Christ. Heavenly Father chose Jesus to be our Savior from the beginning—before the earth was made (see Moses 4:2).

✶⁺ MAKE MAN IN OUR IMAGE

This means that we look like our Heavenly Parents, just as we look like our earthly parents. This also tells us that Heavenly Father has a body with arms and legs and hands and feet and hair, just as we do. The difference is that His body is resurrected and perfect, but ours isn't yet (see D&C 130:22).

✶⁺ LET THEM HAVE DOMINION

"Dominion" means that something is yours to take care of. When you feed your fish or water your garden, you have dominion over them. Heavenly Father gave us, His children, dominion over the whole earth. It's our job to take good care of it and all the plants and animals Jesus created for it.

AND I, God, created man in mine own image, in the image of mine Only Begotten created I he; MALE AND FEMALE CREATED I THEM. (Moses 2:27)

✶⁺ Male and Female Created I Them

As spirits, we were created as either male or female by our Heavenly Parents. Our earthly bodies are also either male or female, according to what our spirits are (*The Family: A Proclamation to the World*).

✶⁺ I, God, Blessed Them
Heavenly Father blessed Adam and Eve with good things, just as He blesses each of us, His children. He gave them commandments to help them know how to be happy (see D&C 59:4).

✶⁺ Be Fruitful, and Multiply
This is the first commandment God gave to Adam and Eve. It means that they should have children.

✶⁺ Replenish the Earth
"Replenish" means "fill" (see Genesis 1:28, footnote c). Heavenly Father wanted Adam and Eve's family to fill the earth with people so that all His spirit children could have a chance to come to earth and get a body.

✶⁺ Subdue It
This is the second commandment God gave to Adam and Eve. To "subdue" means to take something wild and tame it, or bring it under your control. When we use animals on a farm, plant a garden, or build a house using materials from the earth like wood and stone, we are subduing the earth. Heavenly Father created the things of the earth for us to use (see D&C 59:16–20). Learning to control them in righteous ways and use them well is part of becoming more like our Heavenly Father.

And I, God, blessed them, and said unto them: Be fruitful, and multiply, and replenish the earth, and subdue it, and have dominion over the fowl of the air, and over every living thing that moveth upon the earth. (Moses 2:28)

AND I, God, said unto man: Behold, I have given you every herb bearing seed, which is upon the face of all the earth, and every tree in the which shall be the fruit of a tree yielding seed; TO YOU IT SHALL BE FOR MEAT. (Moses 2:29)

✶ To You It Shall Be for Meat

When this was written, "meat" meant food in general. Heavenly Father has put plants and animals on earth for us to use for food and other things we need (see D&C 59:16–20). He has also promised that there is "enough and to spare," or more than enough, for everyone on earth (see D&C 104:17). Part of obeying His commandment to "have dominion" (see Moses 2:28) is learning to take good care of the earth and the plants and animals on it so that everyone on earth will have what they need (see D&C 104:18).

AND TO every beast of the earth, and to every fowl of the air, and to everything that creepeth upon the earth, wherein I grant life, there shall be given EVERY CLEAN HERB FOR MEAT; and it was so, even as I spake. (Moses 2:30)

✶⁺ Every Clean Herb for Meat

"Clean herb" just means plants that are good for the animals to eat. Jesus created the earth with all the plants that the animals, birds, fish, bugs, and other creatures would need for food.

AND I, God, saw everything that I had made, and behold, ALL THINGS WHICH I HAD MADE WERE VERY GOOD; and the evening and the morning were the sixth day. (Moses 2:31)

Thus the heaven and the earth were finished, and ALL THE HOST OF THEM. (Moses 3:1)

✶⁺ All Things Which I Had Made Were Very Good

Jesus looked and was happy with His creations. We are amazed and happy too when we see and enjoy the wonderful things Jesus has created! He created things in an orderly way so that life could go on and on in the earth. First, he created habitats of water, land, and plant life so that the animals would have all they needed. Then He created the animals. Once these things were in place, the earth was ready for Heavenly Father's children to come and fill the earth with people. This careful preparation is one way we can see God's great love for us.

✶⁺ All the Host of Them

This means everything that had been created and placed on the earth and in the sky.

I, God, Blessed the Seventh Day

God made the seventh day a special day when He rested from the work of creating things. He has commanded us to rest from our regular work one day each week just like He did. We call this day the Sabbath day.

Sanctified

This means "made holy," or set apart for a sacred purpose. We are commanded to set the Sabbath day apart from other days and use that time to do things that bring us closer to God (see D&C 59:9–10).

Generations of the Heaven and of the Earth

In this verse, "generations" just means the story of how the heaven and the earth were created.

AND ON the seventh day I, God, ended my work, and all things which I had made; and I rested on the seventh day from all my work, and all things which I had made were finished, and I, God, saw that they were good;

And I, GOD, BLESSED THE SEVENTH DAY, and SANCTIFIED it; because that in it I had rested from all my work which I, God, had created and made.

And now, behold, I say unto you, that these are the GENERATIONS OF THE HEAVEN AND OF THE EARTH, when they were created, in the day that I, the Lord God, made the heaven and the earth. (Moses 3:2–4)

THIS IS the story that Jesus told Moses about how all of these wonderful things were created for us. If we do our best to keep God's commandments and follow Jesus Christ, we will pass our test and return with joy to live with our Heavenly Father forever. This is the good news of the gospel of Jesus Christ.